Life in the Past

Victorian Schools

Mandy Ross

HEINEMANN LIBRARY

www.heinemann.co.uk/library
Visit our website to find out more information about **Heinemann Library** books.

To order:

 Phone ++44 (0)1865 888066
Send a fax to ++44 (0)1865 314091
Visit the Heinemann Bookshop at *www.heinemann.co.uk/library* to browse our catalogue
and order online.

First published in Great Britain by Heinemann
Library, Halley Court, Jordan Hill, Oxford OX2
8EJ, part of Harcourt Education. Heinemann is a
registered trademark of Harcourt Education Ltd.

© Harcourt Education Ltd 2004
The moral right of the proprietor has been
asserted.

Editorial: Lucy Thunder and Helen Cannons
Design: Ron Kamen and Paul Davies
Picture Research: Rebecca Sodergren and
Liz Savery
Production: Edward Moore
Originated by Repro Multi-Warna
Printed and bound in Hong Kong and China by
South China Printing Company
The paper used to print this book comes from
sustainable resources.

ISBN 0 431 12140 0
08 07 06 05 04
10 9 8 7 6 5 4 3 2 1

**British Library Cataloguing in Publication
Data**
  Ross, Mandy
  Victorian schools. – (Life in the past)
  370.9'41'09034

A full catalogue record for this book is available
from the British Library.

Acknowledgements
The Publishers are grateful to the following for
permission to reproduce photographs: The Art
Archive/The Bodleian Library, Oxford p**20**; The
Art Archive, Musee d'Orsay, Paris/Dagli Orti p**9**;
Bridgeman Art Library/Christopher Wood Gallery,
London p**12**; Corbis p**4**; Corbis/Edifice/Philippa
Lewis p**28**; Corbis/Hulton-Deutsch Collection p**15**;
Corbis/Peter Yates p**7**; Fine Art Photographic
Library pp**14, 21**; Hulton Archive pp**5, 6, 16, 24**;
Mary Evans Picture Library pp**8, 10, 19, 22, 23,
25, 27**; Ragged School p**29**; Topham Picturepoint
pp**11, 13, 17, 18**; Victorian Library Images p**26**.

Cover photo of girls reading in school in 1900
reproduced with permission of Billie Love
Historical Collection.

Our thanks to Jane Shuter for her assistance in
the preparation of this book.

Every effort has been made to contact copyright
holders of any material reproduced in this book.
Any omissions will be rectified in subsequent
printings if notice is given to the Publishers.

Contents

Words written in bold, **like this**, are explained
in the Glossary.

Who were the Victorians?

Queen Victoria **reigned** in Britain from 1837 to 1901. People who lived at this time are called Victorians. Some Victorians were very rich and others were very poor indeed.

Queen Victoria

This Victorian newspaper picture shows Queen Victoria visiting a girls' school.

Victorian life was very different from today. Many of our everyday things were not yet **invented** at the start of Victoria's reign. There were no cars, telephones or computers.

This photograph from 1896 shows a horse-drawn bus and a motor bus in a busy London street. 👇

motor bus

Schools then and now

At the beginning of Victoria's **reign**, many children got little or no schooling – especially the poor. By the end of Victoria's reign, children had to go to school until they were twelve.

Victorian schools were much stricter than today. Children had to sit in rows.

☝ Modern children in a science lesson.

School is much more fun today than it was in Victorian times. Now, children are free to explore and learn for themselves. What do you like doing best at school?

7

Little ladies

Most girls from rich families did not go to school. They were taught at home by a **governess** or **tutor**. Sometimes their younger brothers shared their lessons.

inkwell

👆 This governess is reading to her pupils.

☞ This famous painting by Pierre-Auguste Renoir was painted in 1892. It shows two girls at the piano.

Many families thought that girls only needed a very basic education. They were mainly taught things they would need to attract a husband, such as singing, drawing and needlework.

Toughen them up!

Boys from rich families were sent away to **boarding school** from around the age of seven. Their lives were harsh and uncomfortable at school, to toughen them up.

cold water
for washing

bare floor

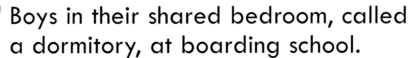 Boys in their shared bedroom, called a dormitory, at boarding school.

Many **middle-class** families sent their sons to local **grammar schools**. Boys were expected to work hard, be clean and neat, and to obey their teacher.

No matter how boring the lesson, these boys had to pay attention or they would be punished.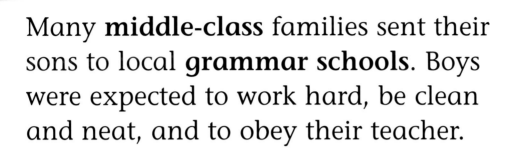

A little learning

Many families could not afford high **fees** charged by schools. From the 1830s, churches and **charities** set up schools with lower fees. Children learnt religion and the 'three Rs' – reading, writing and arithmetic (maths).

This woman is teaching children in her home. This might be all the schooling children would get.

A girl is helping while her mother makes brushes at home.

Many poor families could not afford to send their children to school at all. They needed children to work from an early age, to bring money into the home.

Children who worked every day except
Sunday could go to Sunday school
at church. There they could learn
as they read from the Bible.

This painting, from 1874, shows a
minister teaching at a Sunday school.

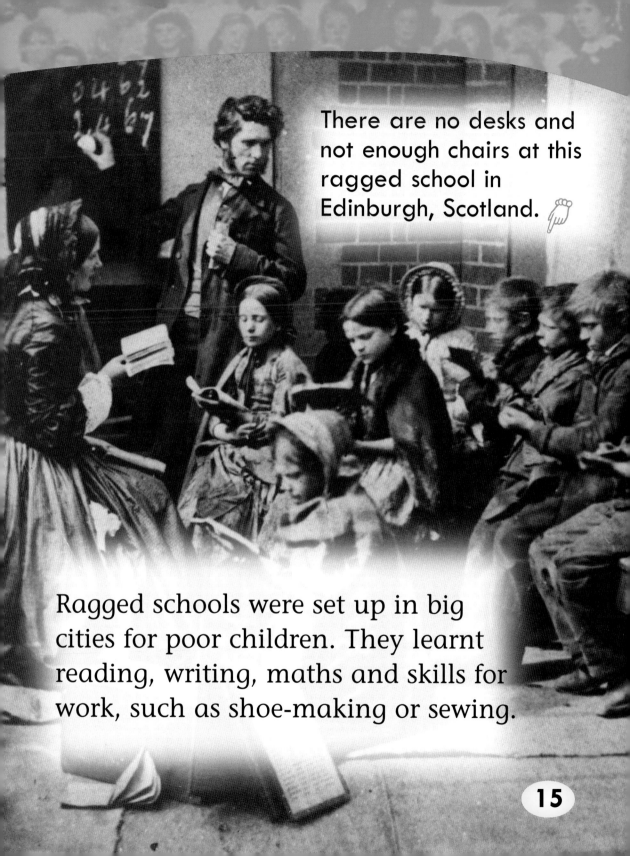

There are no desks and not enough chairs at this ragged school in Edinburgh, Scotland.

Ragged schools were set up in big cities for poor children. They learnt reading, writing, maths and skills for work, such as shoe-making or sewing.

School for all

monitor   teacher

Older children called monitors are helping the teacher with this large class.

In 1870, the government made new **laws** saying that all children from the age of five to ten could go to school. Many schools were built. Some had huge classes – with about 200 pupils.

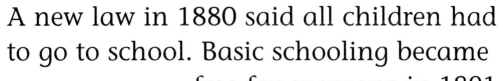

A new law in 1880 said all children had to go to school. Basic schooling became free for everyone in 1891. Children were then taught the 'three Rs', history, geography and a little science, too.

After 1880, children who did not want to go to school were made to go.

In the classroom

Victorian teachers were very strict. Children had to behave well all the time. The teachers worked hard to teach such big classes.

A boys' class photograph. The writing on the blackboard says, 'Do right and fear not'.

This boy is standing on a stool and wearing a **dunce's hat** as a punishment.

There were harsh punishments for children who did not obey their teacher. Sometimes they were beaten for being naughty. Many children were afraid at school.

Learning lessons

What might you find in a Victorian classroom? Some objects might be familiar today, such as a chalkboard, map or globe. There were no calculators or computers, though.

This page from a Victorian picture book shows objects from the schoolroom.

IN THE SCHOOL-ROOM.

The Bench and Desk. The Map. The Note-book. The Reading-book. The Globe. The Chalk. The Compass. The Sponge. The Ink-bottle. The Violin. The Steel-pen. The Black-board. The Pen-knife. The Chair. The Pencil-box. The Ruler. The Easel. The Slate. The Penholder. The Button-hook. The Tri-angle. The Knitting-ball. The Exercise-book. The Pencil. The Book. The Satchel. The Bible. The Counting-machine. The Drawing-board. The Yard-measure. The Pointer.

Victorian children wrote by scratching on a **slate**. The slate could be wiped clean to use again. Mostly children learnt lessons by heart, or copied from the blackboard.

Here are some sayings which Victorian children might have copied:

'A fool and his money are soon parted.'

'Waste not, want not.'

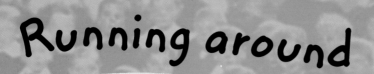

Running around

Like other lessons, sport or PE was strict. Children stood in long lines in the playground to do exercises, called drill, together.

These Victorian boys are doing exercises in a foggy school playground.

Victorian schools did not have playtime, like schools today. Children played together before and after school. There were no adults in charge, so bigger children often bullied smaller ones.

Learning for life

Once they were past the age of ten, the lives of rich and poor children became even more different. Children from richer families might go to **grammar schools**. A lucky few might go on to university.

This school photograph from 1880 shows grammar school boys wearing medals for being good.

washing board

flat iron   laundry tubs

These girls are learning how to iron collars and cuffs in London, England.

Instead, poorer children learned skills for work and life, such as woodwork or **laundry**. This was to help them to earn their living.

Adults at school

Many adults who had not learned much at school wanted to educate themselves. New, free public libraries were opened so that people could borrow books to read.

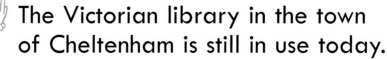 The Victorian library in the town of Cheltenham is still in use today.

Trades unions, libraries and other organizations put on evening classes for adults. Many men and women learnt new skills and got better jobs.

slate

chalkboard

teacher

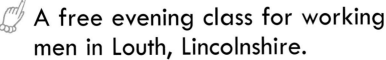
A free evening class for working men in Louth, Lincolnshire.

Let's find out!

Many Victorian school buildings are still in use today. Can you find out when your school was built? Which schools in your area were built in Victorian times?

Modern children playing outside their small Victorian school building.

These school children are visiting the Ragged School Museum in London to find out what a ragged school was like.

You can find out more about Victorian schools at your local library or museum. Ask for information about Victorian buildings to visit in your area.

Timeline

1833 Government starts school **inspections**

1837 Victoria is crowned Queen of Great Britain

1842 New **laws** stop children under ten from working underground in mines. Government starts to train pupils who want to be teachers while they are still at school.

1851 The Great Exhibition is held at the Crystal Palace, London

1854 British troops fight in the Crimean War against Russia

1861 Prince Albert, Victoria's husband, dies

1870 Government passes a law saying there should be enough schools for all children from the ages of five to ten to go to school. Government builds schools and employs teachers for the first time.

1880 All children between the age of five and ten have to go to school

1891 Free schooling provided for all children

1899 All children have to go to school until they are twelve years old

1901 Queen Victoria dies

Glossary

boarding school school which pupils live in during the week or the term

charities organizations that help and raise money for those in need

dunce's hat cone-shaped hat worn as a punishment for not doing well in lessons

fee payment charged

governess woman employed to teach and look after children in their own home

grammar school school which charges fees and pupils have to pass an exam to enter

inspection to take a close look at something

invent to make something a new way, or to find a new way of doing something

laundry washing clothes, bedding and other things

law rule made by Parliament that everyone must obey

middle-class people who earn enough money to live comfortably, for instance doctors

ragged school Victorian school for poor children

reign to be the king or queen of a country, or the period a king or queen spends on the throne

slate flat piece of stone, used for writing on

trades union organization set up by workers to improve their pay, safety and rights at work

tutor person employed to teach children in their own home

Find out more

More books to read

Life in Victorian Britain: The Victorians at School, Rosemary Rees (Heinemann Library, 1995)

Life in Victorian Times: Home and School, Neil Morris (Belitha Press, 2000)

Look Inside a Victorian Schoolroom, Brian Moses and Adam Hook, (Hodder Wayland, 1999)

Places and websites to visit

www.nationaltrust.org.uk
The National Trust has information about historic buildings to visit in your area.

www.museumofchildhood.org.uk
The Museum of Childhood in London has displays about many aspects of Victorian childhood.

Index

Titles in the *Life in the Past* series:

Hardback　　　　0 431 12141 9

Hardback　　　　0 431 12143 5

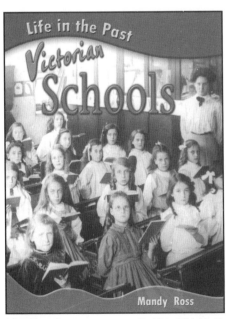

Hardback　　　　0 431 12140 0

Hardback　　　　0 431 12142 7

Find out about other Heinemann Library titles on our website www.heinemann.co.uk/library